21st Century Junior Library

FARM ANIMALS
COWS

by Cecilia Minden

CHERRY LAKE PUBLISHING * ANN ARBOR, MICHIGAN

CHERRY
LAKE
Publishing

Published in the United States of America by Cherry Lake Publishing
Ann Arbor, Michigan
www.cherrylakepublishing.com

Content Adviser: Laurie Rincker, Assistant Professor of Agriculture, Eastern Kentucky University

Photo Credits: Page 4, ©Matthew Jacques, used under license from Shutterstock, Inc.; cover and page 6, ©iStockphoto.com/Lenorlux; cover and page 8, ©Ints Vikmanis, used under license from Shutterstock, Inc.; cover and page 10, ©L. Kragt Bakker, used under license from Shutterstock, Inc.; page 12, ©iStockphoto.com/Silberschuh; cover and page 14, ©iStockphoto.com/Augenblicke; page 16, ©Erwinova/Dreamstime.com; page 18, ©iStockphoto.com/knape; page 20, ©iStockphoto.com/Erdosain

LIBRARY OF CONGRESS CATALOGING-IN-PUBLICATION DATA
Minden, Cecilia.
  Farm animals: Cows / by Cecilia Minden.
    p. cm.—(21st century junior library)
  Includes bibliographical references and index.
  ISBN-13: 978-1-60279-540-2
  ISBN-10: 1-60279-540-1
  1. Dairy cattle—Juvenile literature. 2. Cows—Juvenile literature.
  I. Title. II. Title: Cows. III. Series.
  SF208.M58 2009
  636.2—dc22   2009000680

*Cherry Lake Publishing would like to acknowledge the work of
The Partnership for 21st Century Skills.
Please visit www.21stcenturyskills.org for more information.*

CONTENTS

Cows are very useful animals.

Who Says Moo?

Do you drink milk? Do you eat beef? What animal gives us both of these foods? Cows! We get many dairy products from milk cows. We get many beef products from beef cows. Want to learn more about cows? They are interesting animals!

Young calves are much smaller than their parents.

Dairy Cows

A **heifer** is a young female cow. She is called a cow after she gives birth to a **calf**. A calf weighs about 80 pounds (36.3 kilograms) at birth. But calves do not stay this small for long. An adult cow can weigh more than 1,000 pounds (453.6 kg)!

Cows spend a lot of time eating.

Dairy cows need a lot of food and water to make milk. Cows like to eat hay and **corn silage**. They eat about 40 pounds (18.1 kg) of food every day. They drink between 4 and 36 gallons (15.1 and 136.3 liters) of water.

Think!

Many foods are made from cow's milk. An example would be certain kinds of cheese. Can you think of more foods that are made from milk? Think about what you ate today. How many of those foods were made from milk?

Milking machines can milk many cows at the same time.

Most dairy farmers use milking machines. Machines can milk more than 100 cows per hour. The milk is quickly cooled. Trucks bring the milk to a factory. The milk is **pasteurized** at the factory. This process kills any harmful **germs**. The milk is put into jugs, cartons, or bottles. Then it is shipped to stores.

Cows come in many different colors.

Beef Cows

Some cows are raised for their meat. The **herd** spends a lot of time in a field. The cows **graze** on grass during the summer. Many older cows are brought to special areas of land. They are called feedlots. There the cows eat and grow some more.

Cows usually lay down to sleep.

Cattle need rest to grow and stay healthy. Cows nap about 20 times each day. This adds up to about 7 to 8 hours of sleep. People need to be careful around cows. A sudden or loud noise could scare them.

Cattle are ready to be sold when they weigh about 1,000 pounds (453.6 kg).

The meat from one cow can feed many people.

Beef cows are sold to **packinghouses**. There cattle become the meat you see in stores. Picture a cow that weighs 1,200 pounds (544.3 kg). It can produce a little more than 720 pounds (326.6 kg) of beef. Steak and hamburger are popular forms of beef.

Look!

Look closely at the label on a package of beef. Look for the **sell-by date**. Did you find it? You should buy beef before that date passes. Then you will know that your product is fresh.

Lean beef can be part of a healthy meal.

Got Milk?

Some dairy and beef products have things in them that we need to be healthy. Milk has calcium and vitamin D. These help our bodies build strong bones. Lean beef is beef with little fat. It provides us with protein. Protein gives us energy and helps our muscles grow.

Milk helps keep your bones strong.

Most kids need 2 to 3 cups (473.2 to 709.8 milliliters) of milk each day. Kids also need 3 to 5 ounces (85.0 to 141.7 grams) of meat, beans, or nuts. Lean beef is one choice.

Cows give food products to many people. What is your favorite food that comes from cows?

Make a Guess!

How many foods in your refrigerator come from cows? Write down your guess. Then open your refrigerator and look inside. Was your guess correct?

GLOSSARY

calf (KAF) a very young cow

corn silage (KORN SYE-lij) a type of cattle food that is made from parts of corn plants

germs (JURMZ) very small living things that can make people sick

graze (GRAYZ) to eat grass that is growing in a field

heifer (HEF-ur) a young cow that has not had a calf

herd (HURD) a large group of animals

packinghouses (PAK-eeng-hous-ez) buildings in which some farm animals are killed and the meat is removed and packed up

pasteurized (PASS-chuh-ryzd) heated to a temperature that is high enough to kill harmful germs

sell-by date (SEL-bye DAYT) a month, day, and year printed on many food packages; people should buy the product before that date passes

FIND OUT MORE

BOOKS

Scheunemann, Pam. *Cows Moo!* Edina, MN: ABDO Publishing Company, 2009.

Sweeney, Alyse. *Let's Visit a Dairy Farm.* New York: Children's Press, 2007.

WEB SITES

American Dairy Association & Dairy Council of Nebraska: All About Dairy Cows

www.nebmilk.org/kids/dairycows.php
Check out a cool slide show about dairy cows

Animal Improvement Programs Laboratory: Facts About Cows

www.aipl.arsusda.gov/kc/cowfacts.html
Find lots of fun facts about cows

INDEX

ABOUT THE AUTHOR

Cecilia Minden, PhD, is a literacy consultant and author of many books for children. She lives with her family near Chapel Hill, North Carolina. Dr. Minden grew up in Oklahoma, a state with many cows.